Traffic with Macbeth

The Tupelo Masters Series

Traffic with Macbeth

POEMS

Larissa Szporluk

T|P

TUPELO PRESS
North Adams, Massachusetts

Traffic with Macbeth.

Szporluk, Larissa.
Traffic with Macbeth : poems / Larissa Szporluk.—1st pbk. ed.
  p. cm..— (The Tupelo masters series)
ISBN 978-1-936797-02-8 (pbk. : alk. paper)
I. Title.
PS3569.Z66T73 2011
811'.54—dc22

                    2011021259

Cover and text designed by Howard Klein.
Cover photograph "Moon and Sunflowers" by Scott Bean
(www.scottbeanphoto.com). Used with permission of the artist.

First paperback edition: September 2011.

Tupelo Press
P.O. Box 1767
243 Union Street, Eclipse Mill, Loft 305
North Adams, Massachusetts 01247
Telephone: (413) 664–9611 / Fax: (413) 664–9711
editor@tupelopress.org / www.tupelopress.org

Tupelo Press is an award-winning independent literary press that publishes
fine fiction, nonfiction, and poetry in books that are a
joy to hold as well as read. Tupelo Press is a registered 501(c)3
non-profit organization, and we rely on public support to carry out
our mission of publishing extraordinary work that may be outside
the realm of large commercial publishers. Financial donations are welcome
and are tax deductible.

NATIONAL
ENDOWMENT
FOR THE ARTS
Supported in part by an award from the National Endowment for the Arts

"Come what come may,

Time and the hour runs through the roughest day."

Macbeth (1.3.148–49)

Contents

I

II

III

IV

I

Sunflower

Wind takes your hair
like a hooligan owl
and leaves a deep pocket
of dusk in your scalp.

Love without pride
is a love with no end.
You keep calling me in
to fill up your head,

but the mutinous dust
of the dead yellow field
says better not listen
to a thing with a stem.

Ceremony Turtle

We are born in the bed of the body.
We bear that bed
until the world comes around
and tortures out our flavor.
And what is structure then
but ready grave,
and what is story then
but same sham outcome?
My little face is like a moon potato,
tubes climbing out of it,
beholden to the great
moon potato loser
I gawk at on my back
as fireballs and masks
dip into my murder.
My vest is wrested off—
my heart has tiny flippers!
It buoys up like God,
then boils into garnish,
the tiny thing my life was doing,
fetus of good news
that kept me swimming in reflections
of the hilltops in the lake,
whose sunset crowns
I'm wearing now,
aloft on a blood-red wave.

Traffic with Macbeth

In the eye-water
of the newborn lamb,
a blood clot.

No, a fire-red canoe
heading over the falls
of excess.

And those who fooled around
before ceasing to be
in a garden of roses,

and those who came down,
in a rosy disguise,
with a thud,

afraid of, afraid of—
the heft
of nothing to love.

And those who stayed up,
getting puffed,
puffed up,

like a blimp
without compass
in kingdom come,

or a king
with a king-eating
fungus.

Grapeshot

Once at war, always at war.
Healing? I am healing in the field
by charging forth. Retreat?
Not when the fodder's slopping
through mud, fizzing and flaring
where I chewed as a filly. Not
when the lousy house of a snail
blows its fuse and bursts.
Once a mount, always a mount—
the rawhide balls of bullies
still break with my bucking wave.
In childhood, battery meant
"beating on it." Beating on a thing
to make it work. Truce? I was told
it would pass, whatever it was,
and we'd all sign the dotted line.
When the rye was shoulder-high,
they lit my tail and laughed
while I plowed the freaking acre.
The future ate my boneyard,
but viva, I'm on fire, I'm the rage.

Ladybirds

Brilliance is a carcass
on a snow-white beach.

Envy never sleeps.
I tell my children truthfully:

a long red beard is breaking
from the darkness scale.

He's chasing you because
you're new. Because he's old

and sees the town in dirty tones:
violet sheep and wine-dark

corn. He burns the evening
rainbow like a war-time bridge

until it's charred and charlatans
topple out of robin eggs

and pox your happy window
by capturing the ledge

and chattering like x-rays
that crash into your flesh.

Nihilist

Sullied footprints,
ours (*never cease,*
never cease to move),
and dogs', and theirs,
the star-nosed shrews',
all captured in the mud
on this shortcut
through obscurity; for some,
to end in autumn's
broth, for some to fatten
winter's stew.
If I pushed my face
into the dirt and gulped,
I could wash this shame
a little off. But on these hinds,
above it all, forgiveness
doesn't hurry. I become
the star their nose is
modeled after, its suicidal
know-how, which they
know—there are no
eyes, just destinies,
and there goes mine—
streak across the heather,
hairless wonder who knew
better than to sit around
and apprehend the thicket
through and through.

Nocturnal Council

Who would attack a magnolia?
We're all, not just cows,

blood-phobian.
Ask the mime in the branches.

You can't. You can't—
her hair's in the eye of the axe.

Men the size of a walnut
love to watch anything die.

You keep stretching your mind,
but it's still the same mind,

still in the posse's possession.
You look at your watch and cry.

You were right to doubt the sunrise.
Night is the face that counts.

Gargoyle

A hunter's sickness
at winter's close.
That's my gripe:

forced to watch
the spring of life
and bite my urge

to blow it up
and gulp instead
my feeble dream

of a mauve wet gut
of a unicorn-dove.
On my rash chin,

the barbarian wind
of a sow in manure
about to pig—

the road to fame
is narrow. The road
to infamy is wide.

The cows come home,
summer udders
scored with drought.

If only they would
raid my mouth—
my rheum of drool

pooling through
the marble eaves,
like autumn's sign

to leave my seat
and prowl the dens
of lower things,

lop the duck
and drink the cup
of bleeding neck—

oh lord how hard
to gargle joys
I cannot keep.

II

Rogue's March

We are tied to love and hate—
same track, same train.
Even God fell hard
for heaven's darling traitor.
I think about the stupid boy
who hurt me, how deep inside his hate
was the purest boyish love.
If this is true, if this is why
God gave us reason
only to cross it and cross it and cross it,
then maybe I should jump.
Overnight, great wet things
would tuck me in and praise me.
My broken mind and bones
would join the one-way flow
toward the equilibrium
I tumble from eternally,
my skeleton, a beggarman,
bouncing back for one last drop
of stupid boy—
I tighten up and brace for pain,
my daily bread in knots,
and all those spanking lights and noise
are soft, so soft I'm strung along,
and soft, I grow afraid.

Tadpole

Bitterness, seamstress,
weave me a coat.

My body's exposed
to my watery city.

Cloudstuffs of mold
where once there was belly.

Where is my skin?
How is this glory?

Not only not-frog,
I am forced to be donor

of even my soul,
that flickering ether—

bitterness, seamstress,
whose dummy I was,

I see you on shorelines
twisting my light.

Windmill

I can't cry so I
smack the extent
of my face but I
can't so I hate
the oblique of my
vanes but with hate
I can whish any
bird into gore, abort
any fate, con wind
to kill corn. I wear
a wood kilt. I stand
straight but my head
makes the rounds
of a whore who is
more or less doomed
to feel less and do
more. Sometimes
I pause in an unforeseen
calm. I don't care
what I am. It's drama
I farm, making meal
out of drear by dragging
it on—with arms that
would harrow the hair
on a groin, I man
the horizon, I garland
the void, I castrate
the sun and the gang

of vague air that used to
support me but warped
my career, so I turn
without mercy, I burn
my goodwill
on a purge like a snail
who takes the bran in
and breaks the bran down—
a sanitized foot
on tour in the dung.

Bludgeon-Man

Would that he caressed us
on the road made of feathers
of our loved ones.

Would that we could lose
all semblance of pheasant,
become Mecca in his palms

and overwhelm his senses.
Would that this were dreamy
instead of dull,

this inevitable severing
of daylight into insects
who pad the coming night

with excrement and wings—
would that it were not our life
to augur our own trimmings.

Cold Buffet

The new dew
on the nude
child welled in
her wide navel
like a sad eye.
Here lies the
slapped veal of
neap tide, flat
dollop of dark
vomit. We're all
scared for just
now. Then dawn
and we're off,
our mood served—
a group fish in
thick cast, we seek
the sea's toys
and we coax
our weak thoughts
and poke things
we ought not,
like loose necks
that clout hearts,
or black hats
on bad waves,
the gross risks
we must take
to bring back

our blood day—
*ahoy this, ahoy
that* which turns
girl in our hands
and then grave.

The Face That Promised Joy

Another day in the knee-pine alps,
chewing the creamy grasses.
Day after day of creamy grasses,
why would tomorrow be different?
Her tail is beginning to spiral.
She licks at the hard black lake.
Her joints shiver, and her friends,
where are they? *We're pawns,*
the shepherd tells her, fixing the gun
to her crown. *The more we love*
the world, the more it hates us—
all that cud and nothing sacred.

Rainmaker

Victory has to be rare.
It is the unicorn of all endeavor.

I call your name, rain,
and I fail. I fail and I fail and I fail.

Words come down from wordless places,
rain from rainless air,

mirage from solid paradise,
my salary for failure.

I see muscles in the burning grass,
precipice where thought was,

a far-off purple veil—
and one raised brow, so chalked with loss

that it could be the bastard
of an answered prayer.

Witch-Catalogue

To draw down the moon
when the moon *wants* down—
whose boast's that?

To crisscross the cross?
Flummox the salmon?
My brag's straight:

just to wake for a sec
and not think *die*.
Just to wake, did I say?

But how, from this *what*,
where all eye's stuck
to all dark's palm,

and it's not good mouth
but out of a butt
the next brag's born:

to turn dog on my man
and go with the sun
in a wide open coffin.

Vortex Street

In the clear blue sky,
marriage bells,
clear as the sky for now.
Now is a door.
I drive myself home,
two little clouds on my tail,
one for the body, one for the soul.

I find one window gone
and no sign of glass
or us. Silence at the trough,
our speck of pig-universe,
the slop of our unfinished lunch
where it was—

what could be worse
than a house gouged of love?
Did physics unfix us?
Did forces deep in us
blow up our faces,
pull us down the old tube
we were nothing but food for?

A tube has two holes.
Opposite pulses
move through it.
They make one crazy braid
of unraveling water.

When the drag changes sides,
violence takes over,
and somewhere, no matter
how steady she blows,

a girl is pitched off her swing
by her invisible sister,
and no one asks questions—
the heart just falls out of the wind.

III

Harpy

I sing
one song
for all time.
I've been
not well
but go on.
When they jeer
at my back,
my ears sag
like wet flags.
I choke up
a dark mouse
with no skin
and wait long
for the space
in my chest
to re-fist.
I scythe
without blink
my own cheek,
and my blood
dresses up
the old tree,
and the nymph
steps into
the strop—
and her whirling
feet and her

whirling game
make a crime
in my brain ·
I can't stop.

Fiddlehead

The tip of the fiddlehead,
all curled up.

The rest of the fern
that is trying to live

under the tip that is
curling up. The girl

named So Young
who is turning to stone.

The soundless fern
that is losing its head

to the quiet drop
of its unearned name.

The scream of the man
who is curling up,

about to be cooked
in a tight white

basket. So Young in her
skin that is already

hard. The sound of a spine
in a tongue-tied forest.

Orrido

The trickle, none,
not even ghoul
of long-ago imprisoned
blood, and deeper still,
the moth-filled lung,
the teeth all chalk.
Here the blind have
sight and wish it not
and belly-crawl
to fool the light
that cheats them out
of subtle thought, no
swipe of mud, no
viper skin suspended
on the moss, at least—
all is clean, all is
clean—no echoes of
my daughter's voice
lost in these same
corridors when messed
and moist and young.
Comeuppance. I had
burning-points and
spiral horns. When
taste was gone, Time
ate his children too.
And so did God,
and so will you.

Loosely Related Sheep

The flower life,
at eventide,
falls to cloven ruin.

He turns his face
from Venus, that shiny
jumping bean, and broods

upon the magnitude
of stars he's yet
to chew. Looking

down between his feet—
something sickly blue
astir—his niece,

like sauce, has spread
herself across his
world view.

Edgepeople

I first saw you
through a window:

the thinnest horse
inside a froth

of hair. I squeezed
into that fable,

rocked you,
drained you.

In a sunny town,
one of my eyes

explodes. There it
is, there it were,

your little hand
buried in a starfish,

not your average sew
of part-and-parcel

terror. From where I sit,
my liquored perch,

I love your death,
its far-out nerve—

and then, on cue,
I swoop headfirst

and all our puzzle pieces,
like a million bloody

feathers, come home
in full to roost. In the

jigsaw of eternity,
dying is the glue.

Dunce

I read of him, the man who travels.
I don't travel. Home is in the corner
where I read of wisdom's bosom
spraying milk on someone's chin—
someone wandering a labyrinth,
handcuffed to his demon.
I read of great horned toads whose
eyes bleed open under sudden desert
stress, of muzzled men in foggy
woods who stroll in twos undressed.
Home is in the corner, in this window
where I sit. I look out of glass and
think of fish and how like tanks
a book can press unlike things together
until their faces hurt. I am like a bad
white mold. I fill this corner without
ever getting up. I read of him,
the man who travels, of all the shining
mimicry and seas he sees and then I see
how mental powers can become
tender hills underfoot, or rocky boats
with lusty monks, or one of us—
a drooling child on a crippled stool,
a souvenir of walled-off life.

Mortar

The tulip-red stump
of the princess,
the furred ear
of Evelyn's mother—
in the salt pit,
the kingdom in parts.
Only the barber
is entire, still clutching
his mirror, still
failing to catch her
eye. I am crucified
with slumber. Was
the universe once
vigilant? What
kept me up? I stir,
and down comes this
luminous stuff.

Mouth Honor

Five male crickets
sing and fight.
The loudest wins,

the softest dies,
the neither-nors
fill the air

with mediocre fluff.
The champion thug's
seed's so hard,

his chirp, his sword,
his perfect yell.
The loser rots,

the sweet black gore
of cricket joy
expressed to death

in one dumb glop.
And what if not?
If sounder eggs

were made of sounds
no one sane could guess,
like worms on lures

blacking out
while picking up
a Jesus scent

from big old shells
whose grinning holes
show little feet—

evidence of nowhere
a ghost-wave
won't conceive.

Wish

That there were scissors in this garden.
That their legs were long and golden.
That someone would cut me down
so I could lie with the murdered apples
and turn alcoholic. To be soft and then
cut down hard. That there would be
furze robbing the air. That the curved
roads of orbit, where the moon drops
its shoulder, would drowse my eyes over
with death's green dye. To never know
that nothing is so dark as light aimed
at a dried-out socket. That consciousness
is bodiless, no matter how you slice it.

Accordion

Everything blows, blows away, even fear,
in the wind of anonymity.

The eye of the cat-torn mouse,
its occult gift,
sticks to the rock like a morel,
stem and ball and all.
By summer's end, it's independent,
drained of feline horror.

When the blood leaves my arm at night,
my arm is independent.
I hold it up, my own dead arm,
and flap it at the sleepers
in adjoining rooms around me.
Beating time, like being dead, is easy.

When you hate yourself,
there is one less house
keeping you in, at home.
I'm running amok with emptiness
where there's no such thing.

IV

Sea Lettuce

How easily our loved ones
leave us, speeding into sunsets,

maiming us with absence.
Sailboats, pelicans—

beyond us they don't miss us.
Is sympathy a medicine?

In this green lobotomy,
Mrs. Lettuce, will you listen?

We can be each other's sister.
We can go down whole

into a vegetable utopia
where no amount of man is

who hasn't lost his skin
or children to the knife,

his character to butter—
a massaging, nodding franchise

of ears that take us in
and praise the way we suffer.

Water Bears

We, pawing the edges
of our water-cage
where everything internal
stops. Where the colorless
jello of our unlaunched
bellies sends ripples
to the water's top—in this,
this hideous transparency,
we languish,
our child heads held under
by your polar mother hands.
It didn't have to be like this.
There was light in the world too,
choice in the game of chance:
the teeny-tiny cyclops
drags her bags of eggs,
slave to microbial angst.
But the brain laid bare to Satan
was also home to laughs—
Mom, give an eye to God.
The five of us have forty legs.
In the after-life,
the clowning never ends.

Baba Yaga

I cooked my little children in the sun.
I threw grass on them and then they died.
I sit here now and wonder what I've done.

Death is but a heap of dried-up dolphins
whose fleshy leap and shine we can't imagine.
That's why I get back to work

and listen to my clock and not my mind.
Wisdom ticks against the wise-man
who tries to teach the wicked to be kind

(but my eyes are holes and his old breath
just whistles through the jimson
in my garden). The only seed with stamina

is time. Evening's climbing down
into the cauldron, then rising in the steam
that fills my nose. Ticking, tocking,

that's all I put my faith in.
It's no different to be lilies-of-the-valley
and rub a human ankle with a fragrance

than be the flaky thing that turns it
cold, no different to have ridden silver waves
than be the one to break them—babies,

babies, looking at the sky with so much love.
As I bent to light your toes, the second
split and I was witch but still your mother.

Tantalus Gossips

She rose, I hear, from hell again,
and dove into the river,

grabbed it by its bleeding stem
and shoved it up her private—

Orpheus's singing head
still bringing her to climax.

Love and death, they never quit.
What a gruesome couple to behold.

I'd rather be alone in want
than be between her legs,

beheaded. Rather neck
the airy waif of punishment

than hump the skull
of puppy love remembered.

Cobra

Those dried-up purple eyes,
like peas and jewels and chaos,
watching him emerge,

seeing that he was,
he was, their intercourse,
their torqued and shining son—

then why, unless he did,
he did, he hated it, his head
in egg, the cold blond love

they'd made at length
now in his blood, now theirs
to claim, and so he slid

his hood away, then whipped it
back as fast as wrath
and blinded them with hate

and hate, and underscored,
in two false moves,
that not all brood is grateful.

Octopus

There is nothing for her to hold
and everybody knows it.

Nothing for her to hold,
eight times over.

Pieces of her babies,
girly, ghostly,

float toward her nightly
tossing brain.

Mom has a gene for dropping dead,
but she won't use it

on her misery.
God of Anthony,

god of the good thin men
who starved so as not to suffer

flesh-attachments,
she will give the thrashings

at the end of the long earth day,
she will be the judge

of human carnations,
tying them down

with her windlass arms,
squeezing their hearts to break them.

Jupiter's Doorstep

Time is a vine
in eternity's vinegar.

Goose in barbed-wire,
moon hanging golden

over Vigezzo,
man in a squat

eating his cat.
Cucumbers, dreamers,

waking in soaks,
this is where muses

smear us with presents
no head can hold.

The Fungus

Weeks of no rain
and then rain
and it fills her,
the pin-oak,
her low-lying notch.

Did Christ agonize?
Is the devil really
in the details?

Weeks of just rain
and no sun and the fungus
fattens, like a huge
buttered popcorn,
its orange dermis
pulsing.

My son, missing his sister,
threatens to kick it.
The greater than we.
The less than we.

The edges grow
redder, the interior
deeper, more like an ear
bleeding from rumor,
or more like a sex
with no partner but air,

air with ambition,
air with a method,
air that has screwed her
so hard she can whistle—

the periphery shifts.
Acorns dribble.
Gone is the toy
of her physical sense.

Like a mouth
gobbed with snow
for a month, then it
crumbles. I can almost
hear reason
returning to me,
a decomposed rectum,
an unfeeling feeling—
the bodiless stretch
of the rest of grieving.

Vanished Harvest

They call it a lazy breeze.
Under its slow grope,
trees drop their favorite work.

And pigeons, their pigeon
droppings, and the bleach
that I drop on the porch

because my son might lick one
and die. Because autumn
is sweet on war

and winter is bitter peace,
because the river chased Achilles
for butchering too much—

breeze like a laid-back doctor,
the soul is dense
when you come so late.

Acknowledgments

Poems from this book, often in different versions, appeared in the following journals.

Backwards City Review	"Mortar" and "Windmill"
Bat City Review	"Loosely Related Sheep"
Boulevard	"Sea Lettuce"
Burnside Review	"Jupiter's Doorstep" (as "Blue Ruin") and "Rogue's March"
Caffeine Destiny	"Orrido"
Cerise Press	"Witch-Catalogue"
Chicago Review	"Ceremony Turtle," "Harpy" (as "Cheek"), and "Nihilist"
Chronicle of Higher Education	"Bludgeon-Man" and "Vanished Harvest"
Columbia Journal	"Traffic with Macbeth"
Columbia Poetry Review	"Edgepeople," "The Fungus," "Tantalus Gossips," and "Vortex Street"
Cream City Review	"Cold Buffet"
Ecotone Journal	"Baba Yaga" and "Mouth Honor"
Eleventh Muse	"Fiddlehead" and "Gargoyle"
Gulf Coast	"Nocturnal Council"
Knockout	"Accordion" and "Dunce"
Like a Fragile Index of the World	"Rainmaker"
Margie	"The Face That Promised Joy"
Ploughshares	"Octopus" and "Sunflower"
Poetry	"Ladybirds"
Rougarou	"Grapeshot"
Sonora Review	"Cobra"
Third Coast	"Tadpole" and "Water Bears"

The author would like to thank Kathleen Heil and her colleagues at Seven Sirens Press for developing the chapbook *Vanished Harvest* (2009), in which versions of the following poems appeared: "Baba Yaga," "Cheek," "Dunce," "Grapeshot," "Ladybirds," "Loosely Related Sheep," "Tantalus Gossips," "Windmill," and "Wish."

The author would also like to thank the John Simon Guggenheim Memorial Foundation for a generous grant in 2009, and Bowling Green State University for the FIL which allowed her to complete this manuscript.

She especially thanks her husband Carlo Celli and her children Marco, Sofia, and Sebastian for their love, and thanks her students, former and current, for their brilliant work and faith in poetry.

Other books from Tupelo Press

See our complete backlist at www.tupelopress.org